DRESDEN - YESTERDAY AND TODAY

This fascinating centre of European art and culture is often known as "Elbflorenz", or the "Florence of the Elbe". The epithet was originally coined by the famous 18th century philosopher and critic Johann Gottfried von Herder, who was greatly struck by the city's beauty. The reason is obvious: Dresden's many magnificent Baroque buildings, the wonderful works of art in its museums and the breathtaking setting on the Elbe river make the comparison with its Italian counterpart only natural. Although there are still some gaps in the city-scape as a result of the terrible air raids of February 13, 1945, which reduced most of the city to rubble, many of the wonderful old buildings have now been completely restored.

The reconstruction and restoration projects begun during the GDR period have been stepped up since German reunification. Work is now continuing apace, with the result that the blossoming city is arising again in its former glory, and is very definitely worth a visit.

Dresden is the centre of the Upper Elbe Valley conurbation. It lies in the basin-shaped broadening of the river valley on the edge of the Lausitz granite massif, surrounded by pleasant countryside with rolling ranges

Catholic Cathedral · Castle (Residenzschloss) with Hausmanns Tower ▽

of hills. Dresden Heath lies to the North; and to the South and East the city is bordered by the foothills of the eastern Erzgebirge mountains and the Elbe sandstone massif. Today, around 500,000 people live within the city limits. The Elbe flows through Dresden for around 25km, with a width of up to 120m, dividing the city into the Old Town on the left bank and the New Town on the right. "Dresdene" was first mentioned in 1206, and the first documented reference to Dresden as an actual city dates from 1216. It remained relatively insignificant until towards the end of the 15th century. Dresden's historical importance began in 1485, when the Electors of the Albertinian Wettin lineage chose it as their royal capital (which it remained until the early 20th century). In the course of the following centuries the rulers gradually added the magnificent Baroque, Neo-Renaissance and Classical style buildings that gave Dresden its unique character, making it world famous. A particularly large amount of building was undertaken under the reign of Elector Friedrich August I, known as August the Strong, and his son Friedrich August II (who was also King August III of Poland). Rich silver mines and a flourishing economy had given the house of Wettin great wealth, enabling the rulers to realise their plans in magnificent

▽ *Dresden · Panorama by night*

style. August the Strong was determined to turn Dresden into the "Venice of the Elbe", opening the city to the water and integrating the river in the city planning concept. He succeeded in inspiring a number of outstanding artists for the project. These included the architect M.D. Pöppelmann and the sculptor B. Permoser, who together created the Zwinger complex, a unique achievement of Baroque art.

If one stands on the right bank of the Elbe in the New Town and looks across towards the Old Town one is rewarded by the breathtaking "Canaletto panorama", from the same viewpoint taken by the great Italian pain-

ter in his pictures of Dresden. The view is particularly striking at sunset, with the silhouettes of the Catholic Cathedral (Katholische Hofkirche), the Castle (Schloss) and the Semper Opera (Semperoper).

Dresden boasts a wealth of world-class works of art. In the Augustan period the rulers attracted many leading artists to the Elbe (including the painter Bernardo Bellotto, known as Canaletto), and also purchased a many valuable art collections. These include a number of very famous paintings, such as Raffael's "Sixtine Madonna" (Old Masters Gallery).

Dresden then experienced a new heyday in the 19th cen-

tury, once again attracting many leading artists. Composers such as Schütz, Schumann, Richard Wagner and Carl Maria von Weber wrote important works during this period, and this is also when many of the city's great classical buildings were erected, including the Semper Gallery (Sempergalerie) and the Old Town Guardhouse (Altstädter Wache). Today, Dresden still has a very high-class and varied cultural scene, including an outstanding programme of concerts, operas and theatre.

The city is now the capital of the Free State of Saxony, and both the prime minister's offices and the state parliament are located here. Dresden also continues to play an important economic role. Over a hundred banks and insurance companies have their headquarters here. A number of major companies are investing in new projects, including office blocks and malls with attractive shops and restaurants. Modern Dresden is a hospitable city, with plenty of pleasant opportunities for relaxing, strolling and window-shopping.

Other attractions include romantic steamship cruises on the Elbe and excursions to the many sights in the attractive surroundings. The porcelain and china city of Meissen is nearby, for example, as is the wonderful Swiss Saxony nature reserve in the Elbe sandstone massif.

▽ *Dresden · Skyline with Catholic Cathedral and Semper Opera*

THEATRE SQUARE (THEATERPLATZ)

G. Semper also drew up the plans for the Theatre Square, surrounded by magnificent buildings including the Zwinger, Castle (Schloss), Catholic Cathedral (Katholische Hofkirche) and Semper Opera. His original plan had been to create a forum all the way from the Long Gallery of the Zwinger to the Elbe, but this could not be realised. Even in its present form, however, the square is one of the most beautiful in all Europe. The centrepiece is the *equestrian statue of King Johann* by J. Schilling, which was installed in 1889. King Johann was a lover of science and a recognised Dante scholar. The *Italian Village (Italienisches Dörfchen)* with its Classical facade was built in 1912/13. Today it is a café and restaurant, closing the square off on the Elbe side; it stands on the site of a former settlement of Italian craftsmen and artists who contributed to the construction of the Cathedral. The *Old Town Guardhouse (Altstädter Wache/ Schinkelwache)*, another building in the Classical style, was designed by K. F. Schinkel and built under the supervision of J. Thürmer from 1830–32. It was destroyed in World War II but has now been rebuilt and serves as the box office for the Saxony State Opera (Sächsische Staatsoper). E. Rietschel's bronze *monument to C. M. von Weber* is somewhat hidden away in the eastern corner of the square.

▽ *Theatre Square · Semper Opera · Zwinger · Italian Village · Catholic Cathedral · Castle*　　　　*King Johann Monument (1889)* ▷▷

THE SEMPER OPERA
(SEMPEROPER)

The famous architect Gottfried Semper designed and built the first Semper Opera between 1838 and 1841, in the style of the early Italian Renaissance. Richard Wagner was appointed as musical director in 1843, but the original building burned down just a few years later, in 1869. Semper drew up the plans for the new Royal Court Theatre – including all the interior decorations – while living in Vienna. When he was finished, he entrusted his son Manfred with the supervision of the building work, which was carried out from 1871-1878. The new version of the Opera was built in the style of the Italian High Renaissance. Countless world-class premieres by famous conductors and directors were staged here. On August 31, 1944, the season closed with a performance of Weber's "Freischütz". A few months later, on February 13, 1945, the opera was destroyed again, this time in an air raid. Restoration work began in 1977 under the direction of W. Hänsch. In 1985, exactly 40 years after its last destruction, the Semper Opera was inaugurated for the third time with yet another performance of "Freischütz". Today, visitors can

Front of the Semper Opera with the main gate, the Panther Quadriga, the mosaic dome of the Exedra and the seated figures of Goethe and Schiller ▽

once again admire the exact reconstruction of the original building. The tiered edifice in the form of a wide arc consists of two storeys of arcades. At its centre stands the *Exedra* with its magnificent *portal* structure. The bronze *Panther Quadriga* on the Exedra with figures of Dionysus (son of Zeus and god of wine) and Ariadne (daughter of King Minos of Crete) is a work by Johannes Schilling, the sculptures on the roof of the building are by Ernst Semper. To the left and right of the entrance *stand statues of Goethe and Schiller* by Ernst Rietschel, a reminder of the fact that the second Semper Opera was originally

also a theatre. Four niches, two on each side wall of the facade, contain statues of four other famous playwrights by Julius Hähnel: Shakespeare and the ancient Greek dramatist Sophocles on the Zwinger side, and Molière and Euripides, another of the great dramatists of ancient Greece, on the Elbe side. From the splendid *foyer* one passes through the richly-decorated *staircase vestibules* and walkways to the perfectly-restored *auditorium*, the decor of which is particularly magnificent. Today only four of the original five circles are open to the audience, the fifth is used for the lighting. Particularly noteworthy:

▽ *Semper Opera, Panther Quadriga*

Staircase vestibules ▷

△ *Semper Opera, auditorium and gala boxes*   *Stage curtain* ▽

the *proscenium boxes*, the elaborate *stage portal* and the *gala boxes* flanked by columns. The lavish *stage curtain* by Ferdinand Keller shows the figure of Fantasy sitting on her throne. There are also numerous works of art around the edges of the *ceiling*, and the *five-minute clock* beneath the proscenium painting is framed by puttos. The unique acoustics of the auditorium are another outstanding feature that has made the Semper Opera famous well beyond Dresden's borders. All in all a night out at the Semper Opera is a guarantee of a truly unforgettable experience.

SCHAUSPIELHAUS THEATRE

In 1912–13 the Schauspielhaus theatre was built on the very cramped site opposite the Crown Gate (Kronentor) of the Zwinger, designed by W. Lossow and M. H. Kühne. The architects modelled the facade of the side facing the Zwinger to harmonise with the latter's Neo-Baroque elements. In its day, the Schauspielhaus was Europe's most modern theatre. It was gutted by fire in 1945 and rebuilt in 1946–48. Until the re-opening of the Semper Opera the Schauspielhaus served as a home for the State Opera for nearly forty years.

Semper Opera, upper circular foyer ▽

△ *Kristallpalast Cinema*

Schauspielhaus Theatre ▽

CATHOLIC CATHEDRAL (KATHOLISCHE HOFKIRCHE)

Today, the former Catholic Court Church is the Cathedral of the diocese of Dresden-Meissen, dedicated to St Trinitatis. Located between Theatre Square (Theaterplatz) and Castle Square (Schlossplatz), it is Saxony's biggest church building, with an area of around 4,800 square metres. The monumental church was built in 1738–55 in the style of the Italian High Baroque, as a counterpart to the Protestant Church of Our Lady (Frauenkirche). The construction of the Catholic Cathedral cost considerably more, however. Elector Friedrich August II (King August III of Poland) originally commissioned the Roman architect Gaetano Chiaveri to draw up the plans, but he was then replaced by a team of three German architects. The actual building work was carried out by Italian craftsmen and artists. The 78 larger-than-life *figures of saints* on the attics and in the niches are the work of the sculptor Lorenzo Mattiellis. The church was gutted by fire in 1945, but by 1979 the restoration work was virtually complete. The nearly 90m tall *bell tower* of the cathedral containing the main gate dominates Dresden's skyline and is one of the city's best-known landmarks. One must

Catholic Cathedral (Katholische Hofkirche) ▽

now enter the magnificent three-naved basilica through a side entrance as the main entrance is closed. One of the most striking and unusual features is the broad, semi-circular *ambulatory* around the central nave. This was built to make it possible to perform processions inside the church, so as not to provoke the city's largely Protestant population. On both sides of the main altar are *box seats* that were reserved for members of the royal families. Also worth seeing are the impressive carved wooden *pulpit* (1712–22) by Balthasar Permoser, and the painting of the *Ascension of Christ* (9.3m high, 4.2m wide) above the high altar, by Anton Raphael Mengs –

the side altars are also his work. The priceless *church organ* was built by Gottfried Johann Silbermann and is one of his last and most beautiful works. Forty-nine sarcophagi of the kings and princes of Saxony can be seen in the four rooms of the *crypt*, including those of Friedrich August II and the Dante scholar King Johann, whose bronze sarcophagus is particularly magnificent. Also stored here is the receptacle containing the heart of August the Strong. (The Polish king's body was laid to rest in the cathedral of Krakow.) In 1980 the Vatican issued a decree making the Catholic Cathedral the official cathedral of the diocese of Dresden and Meissen.

▽ *Pulpit (1722) by Balthasar Permoser*

Catholic Cathedral, organ by Gottfried Johann Silbermann (orig. from 1753) ▷

THE ZWINGER

The Zwinger is one of Dresden's best known buildings. This world-famous masterpiece of Baroque architecture consists of a complex of pavilions and galleries around a huge open esplanade. The name "Zwinger" is actually an old military fortifications term that refers to the open space between the inner and outer walls of a fortress. In 1709 part of the city fortifications were surrounded by wooden arcades to create a festival ground. The Zwinger was then built in this location from 1710–32, in a series of construction phases. August the Strong originally only asked the famous architect Matthäus Daniel Pöppelmann to build a simple orangery. In the course of time, this led to the construction of the *corner pavilions* and an *arched gallery* on the ramparts side. The architectural highlight of the complex is the *Ramparts Pavilion (Wallpavillon)* with its impressive sculptures of gods and heroes. Its rich ornamental decorations, along with most of the other figures and ornaments of the entire Zwinger complex, are the work of the sculptor Balthasar Permoser, who collaborated closely with Pöppelmann on the project. The Ramparts Pavilion (Wallpavillon), a work of consummate artistry, is

◁ *Catholic Cathedral, altar with altarpiece "The Ascension of Christ" (Anton Raphael Mengs)*   *Zwinger, Ramparts Pavilion* ▽

topped by a sculpture of Hercules carrying the world on his shoulders. The *Long Gallery (Langgalerie)* with its 36 axes, the *pavilions* on the Castle side and the *Crown Gate (Kronentor)* were added in the next phase. The Crown Gate is also the Zwinger's official main entrance; its attica is richly decorated with human figures and the onion-shaped cupola is topped by a golden Polish crown borne aloft by four eagles. In the next phase the *Carillon Pavilion (Glockenspielpavillon)* was built on the Castle side, as a mirror image of the tract on the ramparts side. The carillon made of Meissen porcelain was installed later on, in 1924–36. Following completion of the restoration work in 1995 the carillon is now functional again and has been programmed with a large number of different melodies. In the original Zwinger complex there were no buildings on the side facing the Elbe; this section was simply enclosed by a high wall. After 1847 this site was used for the construction of the *Art Gallery (Gemäldegalerie)*, a building in the High Renaissance style designed by Gottfried Semper. The sculptures are by Ernst Rietschel, Ernst Julius Hähnel and Johannes Schilling. The Zwinger was destroyed in the 1945 air raids but rebuilt again quickly. The

▽ *Zwinger, Bath of the Nymphs (Nymphenbad)*

Crown Gate (Kronentor) ▷

▽ *Bath of the Nymphs (Nymphenbad)*

work was completed in 1963. Originally, the Zwinger was white and the roofs were painted blue. Also worth seeing is the *Bath of the Nymphs (Nymphenbad)*, a magnificent work of water art in the Baroque style. This intimate set-piece is located behind the French Pavilion and it too is based on original designs by Pöppelmann, although it was actually built in the early 20th century. In the middle of the Bath of the Nymphs is a rectangular basin in which water flows down through a fantastic series of cascades. The imaginative decor (with dolphins, tritons and nymphs in the niches) gives the bath a very lively appearance.

The Zwinger is full of impressive, richly-decorated staircases, and the best view of the entire complex is to be had from the richly-decorated balustrades at the top of the steps. In the past the Zwinger was a venue for lavish and wild celebrations, a seemingly endless succession of sumptuous court parties. The most extravagant festivity, lasting a total of four weeks, was held in 1719 to celebrate the marriage of Prince Elector Friedrich August to the Kaiser's daughter Maria Josepha. Today's visitors can a enjoy somewhat less lavish but equally unforgettable experience: open air concerts in the Zwinger courtyard.

▽ *Zwinger, Carillon Pavilion (Glockenspielpavillon)*

Herms on the Ramparts Pavilion (Wallpavillon) ▷

MUSEUMS IN THE ZWINGER

The Zwinger was originally built as an orangery and festival ground, but it already ceased to be used for these functions in the Augustan period. Ever since then – up to the present day – the main function of the buildings has been to house museums. The *Porcelain Collection* has been housed in the Southwest Pavilion of the Zwinger since 1962; it is one of the largest of its kind in the world, alongside the collections in the Chinese Imperial Palace and the Serail Museum in Istanbul. It was established in 1717 by August the Strong and the original collection was housed in what is now the Japanese Palace (Japanisches Palais). In 1876 the collection was moved to the Johanneum, and in 1962 it was moved once again, this time to the Zwinger. August was an avid collector; in addition to the products of the domestic porcelain works in Meissen he was also very fond of fine historical pieces from the Far East. Today the collection's specialities include early Chinese ceramics (from the 3C BC to the Ming dynasty) and Chinese porcelain (15–18C), early Japanese and Korean ceramics and Japanese porcelain. Also on show are the most extensive existing collections of original Böttger

▽ *Porcelain Collection (Porzellansammlung)*

Large floral bouquet on bronze pedestal (1749, Vincennes, France) ▷

Porcelain Collection (Porzellansammlung) △▽

"The Great Turk" (1740/41, Johann Joachim Kändler, Meissen) ▽

△ *Zwinger, Semper Gallery*

Old Masters Gallery (Gemäldegalerie Alte Meister), Venetian paintings room ▽

stoneware and porcelain from 1710–1720 and Meissen porcelain (including large figurines by Johann Joachim Kändler and Johann Christian Kirchner). Also on show here are the famous "dragoon vases" that August the Strong obtained from Friedrich Wilhelm I of Prussia, along with a number of other pieces, in exchange for 600 dragoon guards. The Semper Gallery houses the *Old Masters Gallery (Gemäldegalerie Alte Meister)*, which boasts one of the most extensive collections of European painting of the 15–18th centuries. August the Strong and his son Friedrich August II started the collection with purchases of major paintings by internationally renowned artists. They established the first gallery in 1722, and in 1747 it was exhibited in what is now the Johanneum. In 1855 the pictures were moved to the newly-built Art Gallery (in the Semper Gallery). In the following decades more major paintings were added to the collection. Today, now that the destruction of World War II has been repaired, the gallery once again houses masterpieces of the Italian Renaissance including Titian's "Tax Penny" (1516) and Raffael's "Sixtine Madonna" (1512/13). Also on show are works by Flemish and Dutch masters, inclu-

▽ *Old Masters Gallery, "The Chocolate Girl" (J. É. Liotard)*

Duke Heinrich the Pious (Lucas Cranach the Elder) ▽

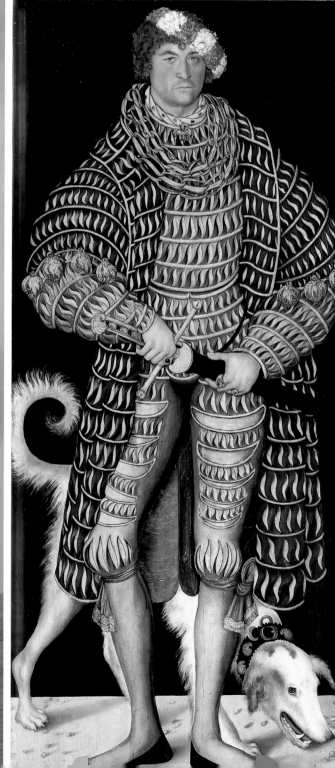

The court painter Bernardo Bellotto, known as Canaletto, painted this panoramic view of Dresden with Augustus Bridge, the Church of Our Lady and the Catholic Cathedral (1748, Old Masters Gallery

Sixtine Madonna (Raffael, circa 1513) ▷▷

ding Rembrandt's "Self-portrait with Saskia" (1635/39) and van Delft's "At the Matchmaker's" (1656). The most important works on show by German painters include: The "St Catharine Altar" by Lucas Cranach the Elder, the "Portrait of Charles de Solier" by Hans Holbein the younger, and Albrecht Dürer's "Seven Torments of Maria" and "Portrait of Bernhard von Reesen". Canaletto's famous old Dresden cityscapes and the "Chocolate Girl" by Jean Étienne Liotard are also on show at the Old Master's Gallery. The *Armoury (Rüstkammer, Historical Museum, Dresden State Art Collection)* in the east

wing of the Semper building houses one of the world's greatest collections of parade weaponry, including parade weapons and armour, many swords and daggers, hunting and tournament weapons and the magnificent dress regalia of the Saxon princes from the 16–18C. Among the most impressive exhibits are the parade armour for horse and rider of the Swedish King Erik XIV, the tournament armour of Prince Elector August and the coronation regalia of August the Strong, which he wore when he was crowned King of Poland in 1697. The *Salon of Mathematics and Physics (Mathematisch-Physika-*

▽ *Salon of Mathematics and Physics, astronomical clock (planetary clock)*

Globe clock (celestial globe) ▽

lischer Salon) in the Northwest Pavilion houses a major collection of scientific and technical instruments, terrestrial and celestial globes (13–19C), world maps and atlases. Also on show is a world-class collection of clocks, including some very rare pieces (sundials, hourglasses, artistic and mechanical clocks, table and wall clocks, pocket watches). The museum was originally established with a part of the collection from the former Chamber of Arts and Rarities of the Princes Elector, founded in 1560. The Chamber's 1587 inventory lists 10,000 items, including 950 mathematical and technical instruments. Among the most valuable exhibits in the Salon of Mathematics and Physics are the globe clock (celestial globe, 1586) and the astronomical clock (planetary clock), which is also a work of art in its own right. The permanent collection of the *Zoology Museum (Tierkundemuseum)* titled "Animals in Cultural History" is also very extensive, with exhibits ranging from insects to mammals. The very large beetle collection and a selection of extinct animals are particularly noteworthy.

▽ *Castle, courtyard*

CASTLE (RESIDENZSCHLOSS)

The former royal residence of the Wettin dynasty is without doubt one of the most impressive Renaissance buildings in all Germany. There are three main courtyards around which individual buildings of the Castle are grouped. The history of its construction spans from the 12th century to the late 19th century. The original medieval fortress was expanded and converted to a magnificent residential palace in the 15th and 16th centuries. Following a fire in 1701, August the Strong had the complex rebuilt with a new design, from 1717–19. The 800th anniversary celebrations of the house of Wettin were taken as an opportunity for another major renovation in the style of the Neo-Renaissance from 1889–1901. The Castle was destroyed in 1945, and reconstruction work started in 1986. Large parts are already completed and the Green Vault, the Kupferstichkabinett (Copper Engravings Collection) and the Art Library are already in the building. The rooms are to be completely restored in time for Dresden's 800th anniversary, and other museums of the State Art Collections (the Armoury and Coin Collection) will be housed here. The *George Gate (Georgentor)* rebuilt in the year 1964 to 1966, was also known as the George Building (Georgenbau), which

George Gate and Hausmanns Tower ▽

connects the Castle and the Stable Courtyard. The original structure was built in 1898–1901 by Gustav Dunger and Gustav Fröhlich. The equestrian statue of Duke Georg the Bearded and the decorative sculpture work are by Christian Behrens. The 101m high *Hausmanns Tower (Hausmannsturm)* restored in 1991 was originally built in 1674-76 by Wolf Caspar von Klengel. The *Long Colonnade (Langer Gang)*, probably built by Giovanni Maria Nosseni in 1586-88, originally housed an ancestral portrait gallery of the Wettins, than became a gun gallery. Today it is used as a part of the Transport Museum. It connects the George Gate with the Johanneum, and the Procession of Dukes was installed on its outside wall. The Long Colonnade consists of open arcades decorated with coats of arms and hunting trophies; the arcades rest on Tuscan columns, and the Colonnade borders on the *Stable Courtyard (Stallhof)*. This courtyard was formerly used for staging jousting contests and tournaments. A number of interesting artefacts survive from this period, including the bronze pillars with the rings that the knights would try to hit with their lances (1601), the jousting course and the Schwemme (a bath and watering trough for the horses). It is the only surviving tournament ground of this kind in Europe.

▽ *Castle (Residenzschloss)*

THE PROCESSION OF DUKES
(FÜRSTENZUG)

The Procession of Dukes is a huge wall mosaic 102m long on the rear side of the Long Colonnade (Langer Gang) running from the Stable Courtyard of the Castle. Together with other figures, it shows the 35 rulers of the house of Wettin from the 12th–20th centuries, with their titles. The 92 figures in the mural also include the most famous Wettins such as August the Strong (shown as the Polish King August II) and his son Friedrich August II (August III of Poland). The original mural was created by Wilhelm Walther since 1872, using the sgraffito technique. The monumental picture was soon damaged by the weather, however, and in 1906–07 it was transferred to 25,000 Meissen porcelain tiles – making it the world's biggest porcelain mosaic. Unlike so many of the city's other great works of art the Procession of Dukes only suffered minor damage during World War II and only a few of the tiles had to be replaced. The cleaning and restoration work was completed at the end of the Seventies, and since then visitors have once again been able to admire the Procession in its original glory.

▽ *Stable Courtyard*   *The Procession of Dukes* ▷▷

Friedrich August I the Strong (August II), reign 1694–1733 ▽ ▽ *Friedrich August II (August III), reign 1733–1763* △▽ *The Procession of Dukes (Fürstenzug)*

ORG III. JOHANN GEORG IV. AUGUST II. AUGUST III. FRIEDRICH CHRISTIAN FR. AUGUST D. GERECHTE ANTON D. GUETIGE FR. AUGUST I

1691–1694   1694–1733   1733–1763   1763   1763–1827   1827–1836   1836–1854

MUSEUMS IN THE CASTLE
(RESIDENZSCHLOSS)

The world-famous collection in the *Green Vault (Grünes Gewölbe)*, started in 1723–29 by August the Strong, is a real artistic treasury, including priceless items made of ivory, amber, gold and silver. One of the finest pieces is the table-piece "The Court of Delhi on the Birthday of Grand Mogul Aureng-Zeb." This Baroque masterpiece of the European goldsmith's art was created by Johann Melchior Dinglinger, helped by his brothers and fourteen assistants. The work consists of 132 figures and 32 birthday gifts, and is decorated with literally thousands of precious gems (including 4,909 diamonds, 160 rubies and 164 emeralds). The *Copper Engravings Collection* or Kupferstichkabinett, one of the oldest collections of graphic art in that it was founded 450 ago, today has in the region of 500,000 items. The collection includes exhibits from several centuries, ranging from drawings, etchings, woodcuts, silkscreen prints and lithographs to modern art posters and photographs. The Study Room is available to private individuals with an interest in art, as well as specialists for in-depth study of the originals.

▽ *Green Vault, golden coffee service*

Green Vault, "Moor" with the emerald step ▽

▽ *Decorative bowl showing the bird Roc and the enchantress Medea*

Showpiece of the Green Vaults - "The Court of Delhi on the Birthday of Grand Mogul Aureng Zeb"

BRÜHL TERRACE

From "Europe's balcony" – an epithet for the Brühl Terrace coined by none lesser than the poet Goethe – one has a magnificent view across the Elbe towards the New Town (Neustadt) side of the river, all the way up to the Loschwitz Heights (Loschwitzer Höhen). The terrace is up to 200m wide, and stretches out for around 500m along the riverbank from the Castle Square (Schlossplatz). Originally, the site was part of the former fortifications. Prince Elector Friedrich August II gave it to his later prime minister Heinrich Graf von Brühl – hence its name. Von Brühl then commissioned a number of artists from Dresden to construct some splendid buildings and lay out a pleasure garden. None of these buildings have survived, however; all that remains is the *Dolphin Fountain (Delphinbrunnen)*, created by Pierre Coudray in 1747–49. In its present form, the terrace dates from the 19th century. A large *flight of steps* (built by G. F. Thormeyer) leads up to the terrace from the Castle Square. The flanking *Four times of day sculpture group (Vier Tageszeiten)* by J. Schilling was added in 1868. The original sandstone figures were later replaced by cast bronze statues. Just next to the staircase is the

◁ The Neues Ständehaus and steps leading up to Brühl Terrace

Sekundogenitur building and Ernst Rietschel Monument ▽

Neues Ständehaus (former state parliament building). It has an internal courtyard and a 50m high tower topped by the gilded figure of *"Saxonia"*. Today the building is the home of the *Court of Appeal (Oberlandesgericht)*. The first building actually on the terrace itself is the Neo-Baroque *Sekundogenitur*. This structure was built in 1896 under the direction of G. Fröhlich, to replace Graf von Brühl's library. Its Latin name was chosen to express the fact that title to the building and the royal collections had been transferred to the second-born ("secundogenitur") prince. Today the Sekundogenitur is part of the Dresden Hilton hotel and is used as a café. Before it stands the *Ernst Rietschel Monument*. The sculptor Rietschel was also a professor at the *Art Academy (Kunstakademie)*, which stands at the centre of the Brühl Terrace along with the *Art Association Exhibition Hall (Ausstellungsbau des Kunstvereins)*. The complex was completed at the end of the 19th century by C. Lipsius in a combination of the Neo-Renaissance and Neo-Baroque styles. Its unusually grandiose design was the subject of heated controversy at the time. The great glass dome – known locally as the "lemon-squeezer" – dominates the group of buildings,

▽ *Brühl Terrace*

▽ *Albertinum*

Gallery of 19C and 20C Painters, "The Cross on the Mount" (C. D. Friedrich)▽

setting an idiosyncratic accent in Dresden's cityscape. The *Semper Monument* between the Art Academy and the Albertinum is the work of J. Schillings. Beneath the steps at the Semper Monument is the entrance to the **Casemates (Kasematten)**, part of Dresden's old fortifications. The *Moritz Monument* (Dresden's oldest monument) at the Brühl Terrace shows Prince Elector Moritz handing the electoral sword to his brother. The *Albertinum*, an imposing four-winged structure, was built in 1884–87 to replace the former armoury. It was named after King Albert, who was regent at the time. Following extensive war damage in 1945 the Albertinum was restored and now houses a number of interesting museums: The collection at the internationally-renowned *Gallery of 19C and 20C Painters (Gemäldegalerie Neue Meister)* ranges from the period of Romanticism (including paintings by C.D. Friedrich) to the 20th century. The *Sculpture Collection (Skulpturensammlung)* includes major international works from antiquity to the present day. Also worth seeing is the *Coins Collection (Münzkabinett)*, which is one of the most important in Europe.

Art Academy (Kunstakademie) - Brühl Terrace ▽

CHURCH OF OUR LADY - NEUMARKT SQUARE

Before being completely destroyed in World War II, the Neumarkt square was the elegant centre of Dresden's Old Town. Once lined by many beautiful Baroque patrician houses, it was also the site of the *Church of Our Lady (Frauenkirche)*. The original plans of the Protestant church were drawn up by the architect George Bähr, who drew inspiration from the domes of Italian churches. Construction began in 1727 but Bähr died in 1738. His successor on the project was Johann Georg Schmid, one of his students, who completed the 95m high Baroque structure with its monumental cupola in 1743. The Church of Our Lady survived the Dresden air raids of February 13 and 14, 1945, but even the massive sandstone building was unable to withstand the terrible fire storm that swept through the city in the aftermath of the bombing. After being gutted from within it collapsed on February 15, 1945. The official reconstruction of the Frauenkirche began on May 27, 1994, and the work is due to be completed in 2006. Stones from the ruins are being integrated in the new building. Part of the financing for the mammoth project is coming from private donations and sponsors.

▽ *Church of Our Lady (Frauenkirche) and Golden Horseman (Goldener Reiter)*

The Church of our Lady (Frauenkirche) ▷

▽ *Skyline with Church of Our Lady (Frauenkirche)*

The new bells of the Church of Our Lady (Frauenkirche) △

JOHANNEUM (TRANSPORT MUSEUM)

This structure, which was originally intended as a stable, was built under Prince Elector Christian I in 1586–91. In the 18th century G. M. von Fürstenhoff and J. C. Knöffel turned the building into an art gallery. After another conversion in the style of the Neo-Renaissance in 1872–76 the Johanneum (named after King Johann) was used to house the Historical Museum. It is the only building of the Neumarkt square that has been rebuilt since the destruction in 1945, and since 1956 it has been the home of the *Transport Museum (Verkehrsmuseum)*.

▽ *Johanneum*

TASCHENBERGPALAIS

August the Strong had this palace built for his mistress, Duchess Cosel, in 1705–08. Christian Beyer, Johann Friedrich Karcher and Matthäus Daniel Pöppelmann were commissioned with the project. The main building was completed first, followed by the west and east wings in 1756 and 1763. Also severely damaged during the war, the palace has now been rebuilt and was reopened in 1995 as a luxury hotel (Kempinski). The *Cholera Fountain (Cholerabrunnen)* was erected as an expression of gratitude that Dresden had not been afflicted by the 1840/41 epidemic in Saxony.

▽ *Taschenbergpalais*

HOLY CROSS CHURCH (KREUZKIRCHE)

The present structure is one of the biggest Protestant churches in Germany, with seating for a congregation of 3,600. It has a long series of predecessors; in 1206 there was already a chapel on the site, which was used mainly by travelling merchants for their prayers. The present Baroque form of the Holy Cross Church was designed by Johann Georg Schmid and Christian Friedrich Exner, and the original construction work was carried out from 1764–92. The design of the *spire* (94m high), which offers a wonderful panoramic view of the city, is by Gottlob August Hölzer. In the course of its history the interior of the church was twice gutted by fire (in 1897 and 1945). The last major restoration was completed in 1982. Fortunately, the magnificent *chimes* were not damaged during the war – the five bronze bells are the second largest in Germany after those of Cologne Cathedral. Today services, vespers and concerts are once again held in the church. The great *organ*, installed in 1963, has 76 registers and 6,111 pipes. The famous *Holy Cross Choir (Kreuzchor)* of the church is one of the world's oldest boys' choirs. The *Heinrich Schütz Chapel* to the right of the main entrance contains the *Schütz Relief* and the *Cross of Nails (Nagelkreuz)* – a gift of reconciliation from Coventry Cathedral, which was destroyed by Germany in 1940.

Holy Cross Church (Kreuzkirche) △▽

△ *Altmarkt Square, the pre-Christmas Striezelmarkt fair*

△ *Neues Gewandhaus*   *New Town Hall, stairwell* ▽

ALTMARKT SQUARE

This square, which forms the centre of the historical Old Town, was first mentioned in 1370. It was a market square and meeting place, and also a venue for lavish festivals and tournaments until well into the 18th century. Totally destroyed in 1945, its main features today are the restored *Holy Cross Church (Kreuzkirche)*, a number of buildings with oriels and arcades, and the *Culture Palace (Kulturpalast)*. The *Striezelmarkt* Christmas market is also held here at yuletide.

NEUES GEWANDHAUS

The "Cloth Hall" (Gewandhaus), designed by J. F. Knöbel, was originally built in 1768–70 for the city's tailors. As of 1925 it housed the City Bank. After the war in 1945, only the outer walls remained. The building was rebuilt over the period 1965 to 1966, then extended, and it's now houses a very stylish hotel.

NEW TOWN HALL (NEUES RATHAUS)

This Neo-Renaissance structure with its 100m tower was designed by the Architect K. Roth and built in 1904–10. The gilded figure atop the tower ("Rathausmann", 4.9m) is by R. Guhr. The Town Hall was badly damaged during World War II; following its restoration, the only remnant of the former rich interior decorations is the Jugendstil *staircase*.

ALTES LANDHAUS (CITY MUSEUM)

The "Old Country House", a palazzo in the early classical style, was built in 1770–76 by F. A. Krubsacius as the seat and conference centre of the provincial government. The three-storey twin *staircase* with its wrought iron banisters is particularly attractive, as are the over 200-year-old cherubs and vases by G. Knöffler. Badly damaged during the war and then rebuilt, the building has housed the *City Museum (Stadtmuseum)* since 1966. The museum's exhibitions cover the city's history from its foundation to the present day.

Altes Landhaus (City Museum) ▽

PRAGER STRASSE

This street, leading from the central station to the Altmarkt square, was originally laid out in 1851. It soon attracted many stylish shops, art galleries, high-class hotels, cafés and restaurants, and the Prager Strasse became Dresden's most elegant shopping street and boulevard. Following the 1945 air raids the street was rebuilt with modern architecture and design between 1965 and 1974, and is now once again a pleasant place for a city stroll.

BRÜHL-MARCOLINI PALACE

The original modest palace was built on this site in 1728. Count Heinrich von Brühl, prime minister of Prince Elector Friedrich August II, bought it in 1736 and had it converted and enlarged, adding side wings and modifying the central structure. The palace then passed into the hands of the Italian Count Camilo of Marcolini, one of King Friedrich August II's cabinet ministers. In later years both Napoleon and Richard Wagner lived here for a time. Many more modifications have been made, and since 1849 the palace has been used as a hospital.

◁◁ *Tabakkontor Yenidze – former cigarette factory*

△ *Prager Strasse*

Central station (built 1892-95) ▽

△ *Brühl-Marcolini Palace*

Mozart fountain (Mozartbrunnen) on Bürgerwiese plain ▽

△ *German Hygiene Museum, the Glass Woman*　　　　　　*German Hygiene Museum, Exhibition "Leben und Sterben"* △

△ *Miniature railway in the Great Park (Grosser Garten)*　　　　　　*The Palace in the Great Park* ▽

THE GERMAN HYGIENE MUSEUM (DEUTSCHES HYGIENEMUSEUM)

The founding of the museum in 1911 can be traced back to the initiative of the Odol manufacturer, K. A. Lingner. The building was erected in the years 1927 to 1930 by W. Kreis. After renovation there are 5,000 square metres of floor space available. As well as the permanent exhibition covering seven separate areas of interest, there are some spectacular special exhibitions to complement what is on offer. The attractive presentation of the exhibits, media installations and interactive displays make the visit a special experience, particularly as well for young people.

THE GREAT PARK (GROSSER GARTEN)

A full 2 km² in area, Dresden's biggest and most beautiful public park was originally created by Prince Elector Johann Georg II. In 1764 it was laid out afresh in the English landscape style, and then extended in 1878. Today the *Zoo* and *Botanical Gardens* are also located within the park. The lovely *Garden Palace (Gartenpalais)* with four pavilions at the centre of the complex is very much worth seeing. The *open-air theatre* in the park is a venue for many interesting events. One can also enjoy a ride through the park on the delightful *miniature railway* (staffed by children) with 5.6km of track.

△ *Augustus bridge and paddle-steamer*

VW plant, Glass Manufactory ▽

"PFUNDS DAIRY"

Pfunds Molkerei, the world's most beautiful dairy shop, is to be found in Bautzner Strasse in the heart of the New Town (Neustadt). This architectural jewel once belonged to the empire of the Desdner Molkerei Gebr. Pfund (the first producers of condensed milk in Germany). Originally built in 1891, it has now been lavishly restored. Artistic hand-painted tiles cover almost all of surfaces in the shop, with dairy industry scenes and other themes. A large range of international cheeses and tasty specialities from Saxony are on sale. Upstairs in the café and restaurant you can enjoy local cuisine.

THE NEW TOWN (NEUSTADT)

Originally known as Altendresden, the New Town on the right bank of the Elbe developed as a separate city until the 16th century; it officially became part of Dresden in 1550. One way of reaching the New Town from the Old Town is across the *Augustus Bridge (Augustusbrücke)*. The original bridge dates from 13th century; the present structure was built in 1907–10, following the historical design. Directly next to the Augustus bridge is the *New Town Market Square (Neustädter Markt)*. None of the important historical buildings on the square survived the War. At the centre of the square stands the *Golden Horseman (Goldener Reiter)*, an

▽ *Pfunds Molkerei - the world's most beautiful dairy shop*

imposing equestrian statue of August the Strong in the guise of a Roman Emperor, his gaze directed eastwards towards Poland. On the south side of the New Town Market Square stands the *Blockhaus*. The original plans were drawn up by Z. Longuelune, but it was actually completed by J.C. Knöffel, and served as the *New Town Guardhouse (Neustädter Wache)*. Between 1978-80 it was restored to its original 18th century condition. The *Jägerhof* is one of the few buildings from the Renaissance period in the New Town. Most sections of the original building have been torn down, however, and today only the west wing remains. This now houses the *Saxon Folk Art Museum (Museum für Sächsische Volkskunst)*. The *Japanese Palace (Japanisches Palais)* was originally planned as a "Dutch Palace" in 1715, and from 1728–36 it was then extended and turned into a four-winged building. Several great architects contributed to this superb Baroque building: M. D. Pöppelman, J. C. Knöffel, Z. Longuelune and J. de Bodt. Like so many other buildings the palace was gutted by fire in 1945. Following its restoration it now houses the *State Prehistory Museum (Landesmuseum für Vorgeschichte)* and the *National Ethnology Museum (Staatliches Museum für Völkerkunde)*. The *Hauptstrasse* leads from the New Town Market Square to the *Albert Square*. In the 1970s the street was converted to a pleasant boulevard; today, the sights here

Golden Horseman (Goldener Reiter) on the New Town Square (Neustädter Markt) ▽

include interesting patrician houses, beautiful flower beds, Baroque statues and fountains. The Classical-style *Kügelgen House* – named after the family of the painter G. von Kügelgen – is particularly famous. Among other things, von Kügelgen earned fame for his autobiographical work, "Memories of the Youth of an Old Man". The house was also a meeting-place for famous contemporary artists, including H. von Kleist, J. W. von Goethe and C. D. Friedrich. Today it houses the *Museum of Early Dresden Romanticism (Museum zur Dresdner Frühromantik)*. *Albert Square (Albertplatz)* is an important traffic intersection from wich ten streets radiate in all directions of the compass. The monu-

mental buildings of the *Ministry of Finance (Finanzministerium)* and the *State Chancellery (Sächsische Staatskanzlei)* stand directly on the banks of the Elbe in the New Town; both were built in around 1900. The *Church of the Three Kings (Dreikönigskirche)* is the most important church building in the New Town. Designed and built under the supervision of Pöppelmann and Bähr, it was completed in 1739. The altar and the decoration on the gables facing the Hauptstrasse are by Thomae. Dresden's modern social scene has now become established in the *Outer New Town (Äussere Neustadt)*. A large number of trendy and unusual pubs, bars and clubs have sprung up here, frequented mainly by the younger generation.

▽ *Kügelgen House*

Artesian fountain on Albert Square (Albertplatz) ▽

▽ *Hauptstrasse and the Kügelgen House*

Japanese Palace (Japanisches Palais) ▽

LOSCHWITZ

This attractive district of Dresden stretches along the slopes above the Elbe, with a wealth of interesting sights. For example, the *Blue Wonder (Blaues Wunder)* suspension bridge across the river between Loschwitz and Blasewitz. Built in 1891–93, it is one of Dresden's best-known landmarks and a monument to the skill of the 19th-century civil engineers, with an overall length of 226m and a span of around 141m between the bridge piers on the banks. The bridge got its name from the original green paint, which unexpectedly turned blue, and from the great engineering achievement that it represented at the time. The funicular railway (built 1895, restored 1995) to the *White Stag (Weisser Hirsch)* district overcomes a difference in altitude of around 99m, running directly to the Luisenhof restaurant, which has a magnificent view. A 19th-century suspension cableway (restored 1991) goes up to the Loschwitz Heights 84m higher up the hillside. In 1880 the painter E. Leonhardi moved into the *Red Blackbird (Rote Amsel*, a former mill) and used it as a studio. Today, the half-timbered complex houses the *Leonhardi Museum* and an art gallery.

△ *Loschwitz – Blue Wonder Bridge (Blaues Wunder)*   *Loschwitz – Red Blackbird (Rote Amsel/Leonhardi Museum)* ▽

MEISSEN

Meissen, often referred to as "the Cradle of Saxony", is one of Germany's oldest cities. The first castle was built here in 929 AD. In 968 Meissen became a bishopric and its city charter was granted in around 1200. Meissen's historical importance waned in the 15th century as it was supplanted by Dresden. The cityscape is dominated by the wonderful Gothic *Albrechtsburg Castle* and the magnificent Early Gothic *Cathedral*. Outstanding porcelain from all periods is on show at the *exhibition hall of the Meissen porcelain factory*, and visitors can enjoy educational demonstrations of the porcelain-maker's craft at the *show workshop*.

MORITZBURG

The Baroque hunting lodge and moated castle is the main attraction in the eponymous town of Moritzburg to the Northwest of Dresden. Duke Moritz built the original hunting lodge in 1542–46, on a site surrounded by lovely woods and ponds. Between 1723 and 1736 August the Strong then had it converted and expanded, creating a Baroque palace with four wings. August entrusted M. D. Pöppelmann, Z. Longuelune and J. de Bodt with the project. Most of the original valuable interior decorations have survived (leather wall coverings, murals). There are a number of interesting sights in the wooded park *(Pheasantry Pavilion)*.

▽ *Meissen, Albrechts Castle and Cathedral*

▽ *Meissen, pewter casting workshop*

A porcelain painter at work ▽

△ Moritzburg Castle (Schloss Moritzburg)   Moritzburg Castle (Schloss Moritzburg), Monströsen Hall (Monströsensaal) ▽

GROSSEDLITZ BAROQUE PARK (BAROCKGARTEN)

This wonderful park in Großsedlitz-Heidenau is the most beautiful in Saxony. It was designed in 1719 by J. C. Knöffel, at the behest of Count Wackerbarth. August the Strong purchased the Baroque park in 1723 and commissioned M. D. Pöppelmann and Z. Longuelune to continue the work on it. The project remained unfinished because of lack of funds, however. Among the particularly interesting sights are the *Upper* and *Lower Orangeries* and many *sandstone sculptures* in the park. The *"Silent Music" steps ("Stille Musik")*, which are decorated with cherubs, are also a very popular attraction.

PILLNITZ CASTLE (SCHLOSS PILLNITZ)

Pillnitz Castle is beautifully situated on the banks of the Elbe at the southern edge of the city. In 1720 August the Strong commissioned Pöppelmann and Longuelune to expand the existing Renaissance palace to turn it into a pleasure palace and later also a summer residence. Working in the Chinoiserie style, the architects added the *River Palace* and the *Upper Palace*, which now houses a *Crafts Museum*. The *New Palace* was built to replace the old palace destroyed by fire in 1818. An unusual attraction in the park is a tree-sized Japanese *camellia* (planted in the 18C) that still blossoms every year.

▽ *Großsedlitz Baroque Park (Barockgarten Großsedlitz), Friedrich Palace with the "Silent Music" steps in the foreground*

▽ *Großsedlitz Baroque park (Barockgarten Großsedlitz), Upper Orangery*

△ *Pillnitz Castle (Schloss Pillnitz)*

Pillnitz Castle (Schloss Pillnitz), Chinese Pavilion ▽

△ *Bastei bridge and lookout point*

View of the Barbarine needle from Pfaffenstein rock ▽

SWISS SAXONY (SÄCHSISCHE SCHWEIZ)

The Swiss Saxony nature reserve in the *Elbe sandstone massif* has an area of around 360km² and stretches all the way down to Bohemia between Pirna and the Czech border. The bizarre beauty of the landscape with its lovely forests, sheer sandstone rocks and columns, imposing mesas and deep ravines impresses everyone who sees it, not just ardent hikers and nature-lovers. Some of the more famous rocks include the *Pfaffenstein* (429m), the *Barbarine Needle* (43m) and the *Gohrisch* (440m). The pretty little town of *Wehlen* is a popular starting-place for hikes to the most famous formation of all in Swiss Saxony, the *Bastei* rock (305m). A path leads over *Bastei Bridge* (a natural rock bridge) to the lookout point from where one has a wonderful view of the countryside and the *Lilienstein* rock (415m). There is also a pleasant *mountain hotel* up here with a restaurant and a café. At the foot of the bizarre rocky cliffs of the Bastei massif lies the attractive little *health resort of Rathen*, which is the centre of lower Swiss Saxony. Overlooking the town of *Königstein* on the mesa of the same name stand the proud remains of what was once Germany's mightiest fortress (9.5 hectares, 2,200m of battlements). The main tourist centre in the Elbe sandstone massif is *Bad Schandau*.

The Goose cliffs (Felsen der Gans), with Lilienstein rock in the background ▽

△ Königstein Fortress

Schrammsteine rocks by Bad Schandau ▽